Landform Top Tens

The World's Most Amazing Mountains

Michael Hurley

www.raintreepublishers.co.uk
Visit our website to find out more information about Raintree books.

To order:

☎ Phone +44 (0) 1865 888066

▤ Fax +44 (0) 1865 314091

▤ Visit www.raintreepublishers.co.uk

Raintree is an imprint of **Capstone Global Library Limited**, a company incorporated in England and Wales having its registered office at 7 Pilgrim Street, London, EC4V 6LB – Registered company number: 6695582

"Raintree" is a registered trademark of Pearson Education Limited, under licence to Capstone Global Library Limited

Text © Capstone Global Library Limited 2009
First published in hardback in 2009
The moral rights of the proprietor have been asserted.

Edited by Louise Galpine, Kate DeVilliers, and Rachel Howells
Designed by Victoria Bevan and Geoff Ward
Original illustrations © Capstone Global Library Limited
Illustrated by Geoff Ward
Picture research by Hannah Taylor
Production by Alison Parsons
Originated by Modern Age Repro House Ltd.
Printed and bound in China by CTPS

ISBN 978 1 406210 94 1 (hardback)
13 12 11 10 09
10 9 8 7 6 5 4 3 2 1

British Library Cataloguing in Publication Data

Hurley, Michael
The world's most amazing mountains. - (Landform top tens)
551.4'57
A full catalogue record for this book is available from the British Library.

Acknowledgements

We would like to thank the following for permission to reproduce photographs: Alamy pp.7 (Royal Geographical Society), **17** (Bryan & Cherry Alexander); Ardea.com p. 21 (Peter Steyn); Corbis pp. **10** (Hubert Stadler), **18** (Dean Conger); FLPA pp. **4–5**, **14–15**, **25** and **26** (Minden Pictures/ Colin Monteath), **27** (imagebroker / Egmont Strigl); Getty Images pp. **13** (Time Life Pictures/ Walter Daran), **16** (National Geographic/ Gordon Wiltsie); Photolibrary pp. **6** (JTB Photo), **8** (Nordic Photos/ Torleif Svensson), **9** (Robert Harding Travel/ Loraine Wilson), **11** (Photodisc/ StockTrek), **12** (Rob Blakers), **20** (Walter Bibikow), **22** (Robert Harding Travel/ Gavin Hellier), **23** (Fancy), **24** (Picture Press/ Uwe Steffens); Science Photo Library p. **19** (NASA).

Background images by Photodisc.

Cover photograph of Mount Cook, New Zealand, reproduced with permission of Photolibrary (Picture Press/ K Nakagawa).

We would like to thank Nick Lapthorn for his invaluable help in the preparation of this book.

Every effort has been made to contact copyright holders of material reproduced in this book. Any omissions will be rectified in subsequent printings if notice is given to the publishers.

Disclaimer

All the Internet addresses (URLs) given in this book were valid at the time of going to press. However, due to the dynamic nature of the Internet, some addresses may have changed, or sites may have changed or ceased to exist since publication. While the author and publishers regret any inconvenience this may cause readers, no responsibility for any such changes can be accepted by either the author or the publishers. It is recommended that adults supervise children on the Internet.

Contents

Some words are printed in bold, **like this**. You can find out what they mean by looking in the glossary on page 31.

Mountains

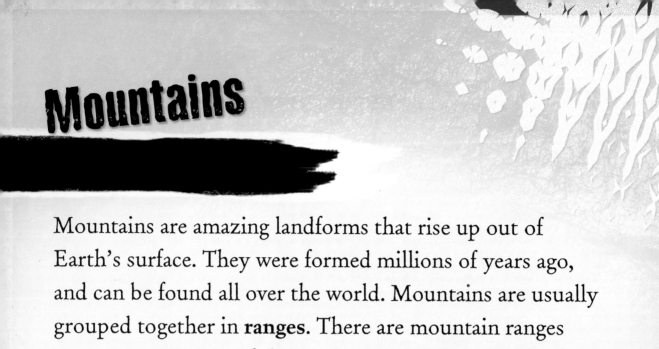

Mountains are amazing landforms that rise up out of Earth's surface. They were formed millions of years ago, and can be found all over the world. Mountains are usually grouped together in **ranges**. There are mountain ranges on every **continent** of the world. One of the most famous mountain ranges is the Himalayas in Asia. The tallest mountains on the planet can be found in this mountain range.

How are mountains formed?

Earth's **crust** is divided into many large sections called **tectonic plates.** These plates fit together like a jigsaw puzzle. Millions of years ago mountains were formed where the plates crashed together and forced the land upwards. The tectonic plates that formed the mountains are moving all the time. This means that the shape and height of some mountains can change. There are many different types and shapes of mountains in the world.

The Himalayas stretch across the borders of many countries in Asia, including India, Pakistan, and China.

Mount Everest

Mount Everest is the highest mountain in the world. It is 8,850 metres (29,035 ft) tall. Mount Everest is called a **fold mountain**. It was formed when two **tectonic plates** crashed into each other and pushed layers of rock upwards. Over millions of years these layers of rock were squeezed together and folded over one another. Amazingly, Mount Everest has not finished growing. The mountain continues to move a few centimetres to the northeast and rise a few millimetres each year.

Mount Everest is the highest mountain in the Himalayas.

ASIA

Mount Everest

Pacific Ocean

Indian Ocean

MOUNT EVEREST

LOCATION:
NEPAL AND TIBET, ASIA

HEIGHT:
8,850 METRES
(29,035 FT)

FIRST SUCCESSFUL CLIMB:
1953

THAT'S AMAZING!:
MOUNT EVEREST HAS MANY DIFFERENT NAMES. THE TIBETAN NAME CHOMOLUNGMA TRANSLATES AS "GODDESS MOTHER OF THE WORLD" OR "GODDESS OF THE VALLEY".

Climbing Mount Everest

In 1852 the mountain was recorded as the highest point on Earth's surface. In 1865 it was named "Everest" after the British **surveyor** Sir George Everest. Many people tried to reach the top of this huge mountain. Sir Edmund Hillary and Sherpa Tenzing Norgay became the first people to successfully climb Mount Everest in 1953.

Kilimanjaro

Mount Kilimanjaro in Tanzania is Africa's highest mountain. This amazing landform is an **extinct volcano** with two **peaks** called Uhuru and Mawenzi. Its location and height mean that Kilimanjaro has nearly every type of weather on Earth. The **summit** is always covered in snow, even in the summer.

World Heritage Site

Kilimanjaro and its surrounding area are part of a National Park. The area is also a UNESCO World Heritage Site. These sites are very important. The United Nations Educational, Scientific, and Cultural Organization (UNESCO) tries to protect areas in the world that are thought to be of value to all the world's people.

Tourist attraction

Kilimanjaro is a major tourist attraction. The highest peak, Uhuru, can be reached without using mountaineering equipment. This makes it very popular with hikers. Visitors climbing to the top of the mountain pass through many types of vegetation, including forests, alpine vegetation, **semi-deserts**, and **moorland**.

Hiking up Kilimanjaro is very popular with tourists.

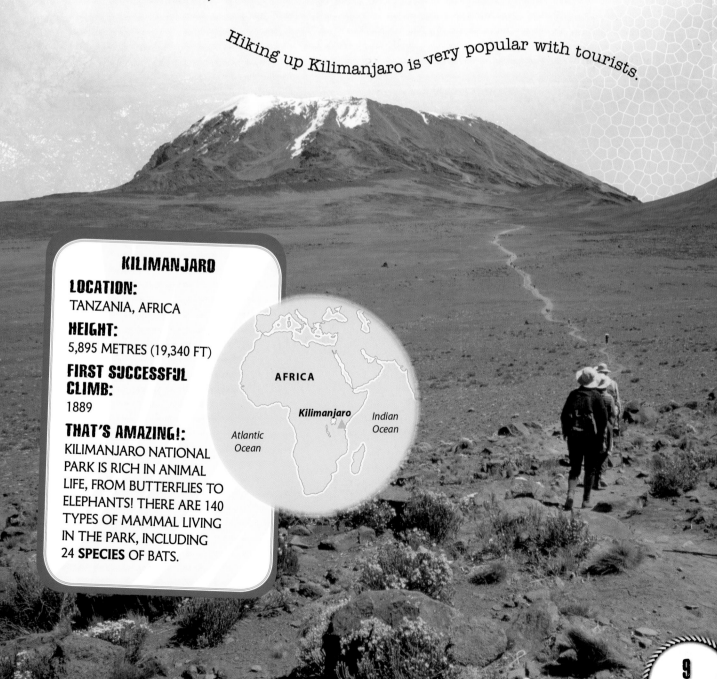

KILIMANJARO

LOCATION:
TANZANIA, AFRICA

HEIGHT:
5,895 METRES (19,340 FT)

FIRST SUCCESSFUL CLIMB:
1889

THAT'S AMAZING!:
KILIMANJARO NATIONAL PARK IS RICH IN ANIMAL LIFE, FROM BUTTERFLIES TO ELEPHANTS! THERE ARE 140 TYPES OF MAMMAL LIVING IN THE PARK, INCLUDING 24 **SPECIES** OF BATS.

AFRICA

Kilimanjaro

Atlantic Ocean

Indian Ocean

Aconcagua

The tallest mountain that can be found outside of Asia is Mount Aconcagua in South America. Mount Aconcagua is part of the Andes mountain **range**. The Andes is the longest mountain range in the world. It stretches from the north of the **continent** all the way to the southern tip. It covers large areas of seven different countries, including Argentina, Chile, Bolivia, and Ecuador.

ACONCAGUA

LOCATION:
ARGENTINA, SOUTH AMERICA

HEIGHT:
6,959 METRES (22,831 FT)

FIRST SUCCESSFUL CLIMB:
1897

THAT'S AMAZING!:
ACONCAGUA IS PART OF THE ANDES MOUNTAIN RANGE. THIS RANGE IS SO HUGE THAT IT CAN BE SEEN FROM SPACE.

SOUTH AMERICA

Pacific Ocean

Atlantic Ocean

Aconcagua

Aconcagua is an extinct volcano. It no longer erupts.

Mountains and volcanoes

Aconcagua is an **extinct volcano**. It was created millions of years ago. Beneath Earth's **crust** there is a thick layer of rock called the **mantle**. Some of this rock becomes so hot that it melts. Millions of years ago, when the **tectonic plates** in this area were forced against each other, some of the melted rock pushed through and formed an **erupting** volcano. Earth's surface is much colder than the mantle, so the rock cooled quickly and hardened. When this happens a lot in the same area the rocks build up to form a volcano. If the volcano stops erupting after a long time it is called an extinct volcano.

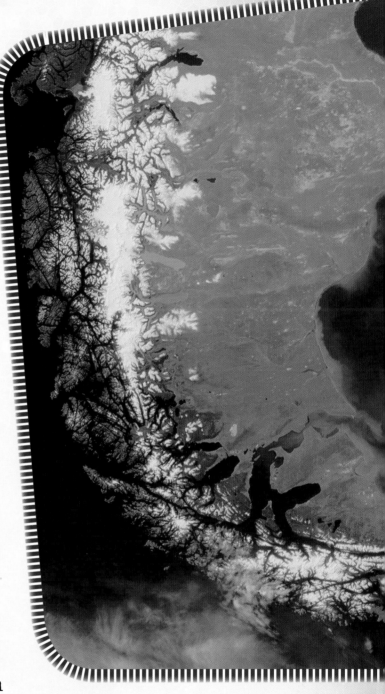

This photo of the Andes mountain range was taken from a satellite. The white area shows the range.

Mount McKinley

Mount McKinley, in Alaska, is the highest mountain in North America. It is 6,194 metres (20,320 ft) tall. The mountain is part of the Denali National Park, and the landscape that surrounds it has a wide variety of wildlife. There are grizzly bears, caribou (reindeers), wolves, sheep, and moose. In the summer the mountain slopes are covered with wild flowers.

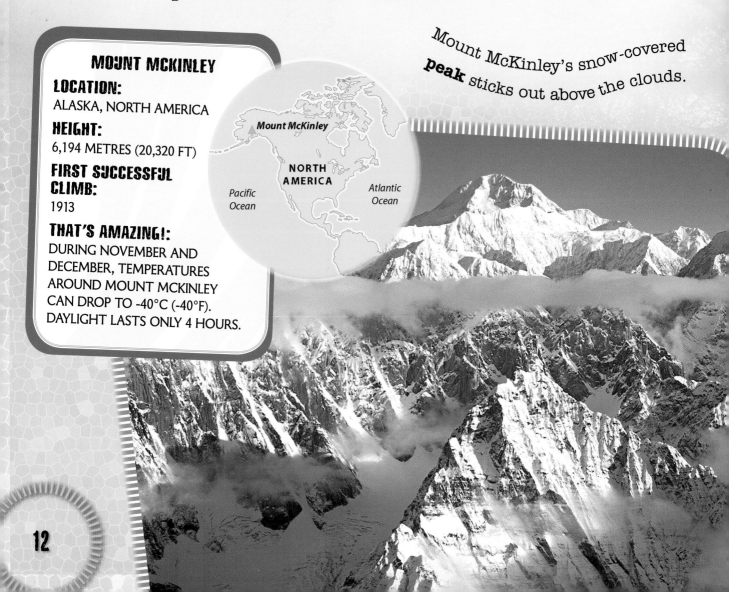

MOUNT McKINLEY

LOCATION:
ALASKA, NORTH AMERICA

HEIGHT:
6,194 METRES (20,320 FT)

FIRST SUCCESSFUL CLIMB:
1913

THAT'S AMAZING!:
DURING NOVEMBER AND DECEMBER, TEMPERATURES AROUND MOUNT MCKINLEY CAN DROP TO -40°C (-40°F). DAYLIGHT LASTS ONLY 4 HOURS.

Mount McKinley

Pacific Ocean

NORTH AMERICA

Atlantic Ocean

Mount McKinley's snow-covered **peak** sticks out above the clouds.

This was the first group of climbers to successfully climb Mount McKinley. Two Native Americans were in the party.

Visiting Mount McKinley

Visitors to the national park can enjoy sightseeing, hiking, and mountaineering. Mount McKinley is not the toughest mountain to climb, but the weather can be **severe**. Many lives have been lost attempting the climb.

Mount Cook

The Southern Alps stretch along the western coast of New Zealand's South Island. This mountain **range** is the highest in Australasia, and the tallest **peak** is Mount Cook. This mountain is the highest point in New Zealand and is part of the Aoraki Mount Cook National Park. All year round the top of the mountain is covered in snow, and surrounded by huge masses of ice called **glaciers**.

Mount Cook reaches even higher than the clouds!

AUSTRALASIA

Pacific Ocean

Mount Cook

NEW ZEALAND

MOUNT COOK

LOCATION:
NEW ZEALAND, AUSTRALASIA

HEIGHT:
3,754 METRES (12,316 FT)

FIRST SUCCESSFUL CLIMB:
1894

THAT'S AMAZING!:
MOUNT COOK IS THE MOUNTAIN THAT SIR EDMUND HILLARY TRAINED ON BEFORE CLIMBING MOUNT EVEREST.

Nature's forces

Tectonic plates pushing together below Earth's surface created the Southern Alps. These forces are still shaping Mount Cook. The mountain rises about one centimetre (0.4 inches) each year. Other forces also affect the mountain, such as strong winds. In 1991, for example, a **landslide** caused by unusually strong winds caused part of the mountain to collapse, and decreased its height by 10 metres (3 ft).

Cloud Piercer

Mount Cook is named after the British explorer Captain James Cook, but it is also known as Aoraki (or Aorangi) from the **Maori** for "Cloud Piercer".

Mount Vinson

Mount Vinson is in Antarctica. It is massive, and stretches 21 km (13 miles) in length and 13 km (8 miles) in width. The mountain is made up of a group of connected **peaks,** the highest of which rises to nearly 5,000 metres (16,400 ft). It is the highest peak on the **continent,** and the most remote mountain on Earth.

Naming the mountain

Mount Vinson was named after the American politician, Carl Vinson. He was a strong supporter of the Antarctic research expeditions.

Visitors to Mount Vinson have to arrive by aeroplane! The views from the sky are amazing.

Deep freeze

There is not much wildlife on Mount Vinson. The largest Antarctic animals found inland are **invertebrates** that are only a few millimetres in size. These animals, mites, ticks, and nematode worms can survive the low temperatures in the winter by becoming frozen in ice under rocks and stones. Although no one lives in this area, scientists do visit Mount Vinson to carry out research.

These scientists are at their camp near Mount Vinson.

MOUNT VINSON

LOCATION:
ANTARCTICA

HEIGHT:
4,897 METRES (16,066 FT)

FIRST SUCCESSFUL CLIMB:
1966

THAT'S AMAZING!:
DESPITE HAVING 24 HOURS OF SUNLIGHT A DAY IN THE SUMMER, THE AVERAGE TEMPERATURE AROUND MOUNT VINSON IS ONLY -29°C (-20°F).

Mount Vinson

ANTARCTICA

Southern Ocean

Mount Elbrus

Mount Elbrus, in Russia, is an **extinct volcano**. It last **erupted** around AD 50, and its **crater** is now filled with ice and snow. The mountain has two main **peaks**, the Western **summit** at 5,642 metres (18,510 ft) and the Eastern summit at 5,595 metres (18,356 ft). Mount Elbrus has more than 20 **glaciers** on its slopes.

Deadly mountain

Mount Elbrus is one of the most deadly mountains to climb because of its very changeable weather. Sudden storms and extremely cold weather are very common. There were 48 deaths recorded in 2004 alone.

In this photo of Elbrus' twin peaks the weather is calm. It could soon change, though.

MOUNT ELBRUS

LOCATION:
RUSSIA

HEIGHT:
5,642 METRES
(18,510 FT)

FIRST SUCCESSFUL CLIMB:
1874

THAT'S AMAZING!:
THE CRATER AT THE PEAK OF MOUNT ELBRUS IS NEARLY 400 METRES (1,312 FT) WIDE.

ASIA

EUROPE   *Mount Elbrus*

Indian Ocean

This is an aerial view of Elbrus' massive crater, formed by the extinct volcano.

The Caucasus mountains

Mount Elbrus is part of the Caucasus mountain **range**, which is known as the border between Europe and Asia. The range is about 1,200 km (746 miles) long.

Table Mountain

Not all mountains look the same. Table Mountain in South Africa is a very unusual mountain because of its flat-topped shape. This flat top is known as a **plateau**. On each side of Table Mountain's plateau there is a **peak**: Devil's Peak and Lion's Head. Table Mountain has its own cloud cover, which can arrive very quickly. Because of the way the cloud looks it is known as the "table cloth".

Cable car

Visitors can take a cable car all the way to the **summit** of Table Mountain. The Table Mountain cableway is South Africa's third most popular tourist attraction!

Here is Table Mountain, with its famous "table cloth" cloud cover.

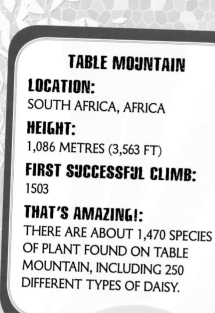

TABLE MOUNTAIN

LOCATION:
SOUTH AFRICA, AFRICA

HEIGHT:
1,086 METRES (3,563 FT)

FIRST SUCCESSFUL CLIMB:
1503

THAT'S AMAZING!:
THERE ARE ABOUT 1,470 SPECIES
OF PLANT FOUND ON TABLE
MOUNTAIN, INCLUDING 250
DIFFERENT TYPES OF DAISY.

AFRICA

Atlantic
Ocean

Indian
Ocean

Table Mountain

The Table Mountain Ghost Frog can only be found in the wild on Table Mountain.

Unusual animals

Table Mountain is home to many **species** that are found and survive only in the amazing **ecosystem** of the mountain. Animals such as baboons and porcupines live here, as well as furry rodents called Rock Dassies. These little creatures look like plump rabbits without ears. The Table Mountain Ghost Frog is an example of an animal found in no other place on Earth.

Matterhorn

The Matterhorn is probably the most famous mountain in the Alps mountain **range**, in Europe. It is the highest **peak** in the Alps. The Matterhorn has four sides, facing the four compass points. The faces are steep, and only small patches of snow and ice cling to them. **Avalanches** send the snow down to collect on the **glaciers** at the bottom of each face.

The unusual shape of the Matterhorn is easily recognizable.

MATTERHORN

LOCATION:
ITALY AND SWITZERLAND, EUROPE

HEIGHT:
4,478 METRES (14,692 FT)

FIRST SUCCESSFUL CLIMB:
1865

THAT'S AMAZING!:
THE MATTERHORN IS VERY POPULAR WITH TOURISTS AND SKIERS. IT HAS THE HIGHEST CABLEWAY IN EUROPE AT NEARLY 4,000 METRES (13,123 FT).

EUROPE

Matterhorn

Atlantic Ocean

Stormy weather

The Matterhorn's horn-shaped **summit** looks like a one-off peak but it is actually the end of a mountain **ridge**. Because the mountain is on its own, it sometimes has its own weather, which can change very quickly. It is possible for a storm to be raging on the Matterhorn when conditions in the rest of the area are calm.

K2 – Mount Godwin-Austen

K2, also known as Mount Godwin-Austen, is the second highest mountain in the world. It is part of the Karakorum mountain **range**, and is not far from Mount Everest in the Himalayas. K2 is a rugged, rocky mountain that reaches up to 6,000 metres (20,000 ft). Above this, snow covers the mountain for over 2,500 metres (8,202 ft) up to its **peak**.

Naming K2

The mountain was named Mount Godwin-Austen after the peak's first **surveyor**, Colonel H.H. Godwin-Austen. It is usually known as K2.

This is the snow-covered peak of K2 in the Karakorum mountain range.

K2

LOCATION:
PAKISTAN AND CHINA, ASIA

HEIGHT:
8,611 METRES (28,251 FT)

FIRST SUCCESSFUL CLIMB:
1954

THAT'S AMAZING!:
THE MOUNTAIN IS CALLED K2 BECAUSE WHEN GEOGRAPHERS FIRST STARTED MAPPING THE KARAKORUM RANGE IT WAS THE SECOND PEAK THEY RECORDED ("K" FOR KARAKORUM AND "2" FOR "2ND").

ASIA

K2 – Mount Godwin-Austen

Pacific Ocean

Indian Ocean

Savage Mountain

K2 is known as "the Savage Mountain" because it is thought to be one of the world's most difficult and dangerous mountains to climb. The first attempt to climb it was in 1902, but the first successful climb did not take place until 1954.

A brave mountain climber attempts the dangerous climb to the top of K2.

Mountains in danger

Tourists have been encouraged to explore many of the world's mountains. People are attracted by the beautiful scenery and wildlife. There is also the challenge of climbing or hiking in remote or dangerous places. Many other people live near or on mountains, relying on them for food and shelter.

This beautiful scene from the Himalayas shows healthy animals and clean water. It is very important that areas like this are protected.

As the number of people visiting and living on mountains has increased, so has the negative effect on the environment. Forests have been cut down to clear the way for roads to be built. When forests are cut down, many animals lose their homes. Also, without the roots of trees to hold the soil together, devastating **landslides** and **avalanches** are more likely.

Helping mountains

Visitors who want to climb Mount McKinley must pay a special fee. This money helps keep the mountain environment clean. In many countries, governments create national parks to protect mountain areas. This means that the beautiful scenery, animals, and plants will be there for us all to enjoy for many years to come.

Mountain facts and figures

There are mountains all over the world. Some mountains were created by volcanoes. Some are over 25 million years old. Which mountain do you think is the most amazing?

This map of the world shows all the mountains described in this book.

Arctic Ocean

Mount McKinley

NORTH AMERICA

EUROPE

ASIA

Matterhorn

Mount Elbrus

K2 – Mount Godwin-Austen

Mount Everest

Atlantic Ocean

AFRICA

Pacific Ocean

Kilimanjaro

SOUTH AMERICA

Pacific Ocean

Indian Ocean

AUSTRALASIA

Aconcagua

Table Mountain

Southern Ocean

Mount Cook

Mount Vinson

ANTARCTICA

MOUNT EVEREST

HEIGHT:
8,850 METRES
(29,035 FT)

FIRST SUCCESSFUL CLIMB:
1953

KILIMANJARO

HEIGHT:
5,895 METRES
(19,340 FT)

FIRST SUCCESSFUL CLIMB:
1889

ACONCAGUA

HEIGHT:
6,959 METRES
(22,831 FT)

FIRST SUCCESSFUL CLIMB:
1897

MOUNT MCKINLEY

HEIGHT:
6,194 METRES
(20,320 FT)

FIRST SUCCESSFUL CLIMB:
1913

MOUNT COOK

HEIGHT:
3,754 METRES
(12,316 FT)

FIRST SUCCESSFUL CLIMB:
1894

MOUNT VINSON

HEIGHT:
4,897 METRES
(16,066 FT)

FIRST SUCCESSFUL CLIMB:
1966

MOUNT ELBRUS

HEIGHT:
5,642 METRES
(18,510 FT)

FIRST SUCCESSFUL CLIMB:
1874

TABLE MOUNTAIN

HEIGHT:
1,086 METRES
(3,563 FT)

FIRST SUCCESSFUL CLIMB:
1503

MATTERHORN

HEIGHT:
4,478 METRES
(14,692 FT)

FIRST SUCCESSFUL CLIMB:
1865

K2

HEIGHT:
8,611 METRES
(28,251 FT)

FIRST SUCCESSFUL CLIMB:
1954

Find out more

Books to read

I Wonder Why Mountains Have Snow on Top: and other questions about mountains, Jackie Gaff (Kingfisher Books, 2004)

Mapping Earthforms: Mountains, Catherine Chambers and Nicholas Lapthorn (Heinemann Library, 2007)

Step-Up Geography: The Mountain Environment, Claire Hibbert (Evans Brothers, 2005)

Websites

National Geographic
www.nationalgeographic.org

Use this site to search for mountains and to find out more about the wildlife that lives on and around them.

Peakware World Mountain Encyclopedia
www.peakware.com

See photos of mountains, and people hiking and climbing mountains around the world.

The Mountain Institute
www.mountain.org

Find out about the people who live and work on and around mountains.

Glossary

avalanche large fall of rocks or snow down the side of a mountain

continent continuous land mass. There are seven continents on Earth.

crater bowl-shaped opening at the top of a mountain or volcano

crust hard outer layer of Earth

ecosystem community of living things and the place they live in

erupt when lava, ash, or rock bursts out of a volcano

extinct volcano volcano that has not erupted for millions of years and is not expected to erupt in the future

fold mountain mountain formed when layers of rocks are pushed together and fold over one another

glacier river of ice that flows slowly down a mountain

invertebrate animal without a backbone. Insects, jellyfish, and crabs are all invertebrates.

landslide large fall of soil or rocks down the side of a mountain

mantle layer of hot, molten rock that lies below Earth

Maori native people of New Zealand

moorland area of open land, usually covered with grasses, heather, and moss

peak highest point of a mountain

plateau area of high, flat ground that often lies between mountains

prospector someone who searches for mineral deposits

range row or group of mountains formed at the same time and in a similar way

ridge long, narrow peak

semi-desert area that is dry, but not dry enough to be counted as a true desert

severe very harsh conditions

species particular type of living thing

summit highest point of a hill or mountain

surveyor person who examines the condition of land or buildings

tectonic plate huge piece of Earth's crust

Index